Artful, but si[...]
fresh. This b[...] [...] passages sing. It
well repays the time it takes to read it. And it's small
enough to share often.

Mark Dever
Pastor, Capitol Hill Baptist Church, Washington DC

The cross is the center of the Christian life and
message. Any time we think of Christ we think of the
cross. But what does it mean? And how does that
apply to our lives? This little book will help explain
that to interested readers.

Joshua W. Moody
Senior Pastor, College Church
Wheaton, Illinois

The crucifixion of Jesus – an insignificant event or the
epicenter of history? Dr. Ryken in his striking exploration
of this question shows the many facets of the Bible's
teaching on the cross. Jesus' identity and mission shine
out clearly. This book will be interesting and helpful for
Christians and non-Christians alike.

W. Robert Godfrey
President and Professor of Church History
Westminster Seminary, Escondido, California

The message of the cross has many features that are
culturally distant to every generation. It is also so profound
that believers will keep discovering rich new levels of truth
about it as long they live. Therefore we need to regularly
reflect on the cross. This book is an excellent aid to such
reflection because it presents deep and profound insights
into the cross written in a spiritually enriching way. It is
also a good book to give as an introduction to the cross
to one unfamiliar with its message.

Ajith Fernando
Teaching Director, Youth for Christ, Sri Lanka

As practical as it is profound, *Salvation by Crucifixion* explains why the cross is at the heart of the Christian faith, and exalts the Christ who willingly ascended that cross to secure salvation for His people. It is a book that will encourage the believer and challenge the unbeliever as it displays the nature of God's redeeming love.

Robert Norris
Senior Pastor, Fourth Presbyterian Church
Bethesda, Maryland

Phil Ryken's book brings us to our knees before the Lamb that was slain. He shocks us, challenges us, and comforts us with Christ crucified. Whether you are new to Christianity or a mature believer, there is no better place to be than at the foot of the cross. Read this book slowly, prayerfully, meditatively, and let its amazing truths penetrate the depth of your soul.

Joel R. Beeke
President, Puritan Reformed Theological Seminary
Grand Rapids, Michigan

Perfect for a thoughtful person who wants to know Christ and discover what it means to trust in Him.

Get this book and give it away (OR get two and give one away).

Colin S. Smith
Senior Pastor, The Orchard Evangelical Free Church
and President of Unlocking the Bible
Arlington, Illinois

SALVATION BY CRUCIFIXION

PHILIP GRAHAM RYKEN

CHRISTIAN
FOCUS

Dr Ryken is president of Wheaton College in Wheaton, Illinois. Prior to that he was Senior Minister of Tenth Presbyterian Church, Philadelphia, Pennsylvania. He is also a prolific author and a member of The Gospel Coalition and The Alliance of Confessing Evangelicals, blogging on their website www.reformation21.org.

Copyright © Philip G. Ryken 2014

paperback ISBN 978-1-78191-307-9
epub ISBN 978-1-78191-334-5
Mobi ISBN 978-1-78191-335-2

Published in 2014
by
Christian Focus Publications, Ltd.
Geanies House, Fearn, Ross-shire,
IV20 1TW, Scotland, United Kingdom.
www.christianfocus.com

Cover design by Daniel van Straaten

Printed by Nørhaven, Denmark

CONTENTS

Preface

Before you read *Salvation by Crucifixion*, it may help you to know something about its history.

To begin at the beginning, in 1995 I joined the preaching ministry of Philadelphia's Tenth Presbyterian Church. In those days I had the rare privilege of serving with the late James Montgomery Boice, a renowned preacher and Christian author whose life has left a permanent imprint on my ministry.

Both of us had a commitment to reaching the city with the gospel. We wanted to help people who lived and worked in Philadelphia understand the basic message of Christianity, which is the forgiveness of sins through the crucifixion of Jesus Christ and the gift of eternal life through His resurrection.

It was Dr. Boice who suggested reviving an old tradition that might help us reach city people with the gospel. Many decades before, Tenth Church had held evangelistic services at lunchtime every Friday leading up to Easter. We agreed to renew this practice in 1996 by holding seven worship services in which we would give short messages on the death of Christ.

I have sweet memories of those simple worship services. We began each week at a quarter past noon, which gave business people and many others time to walk to the church during their lunch hour. Church members and their invited friends would quietly slip into the magnificent Byzantine interior of Tenth's sanctuary and find their place in one of the pews.

Each worshiper would receive a bulletin with the order of service. In addition to a reading from the Bible, the bulletin offered thought-provoking quotations from sacred and secular sources, introducing the theme for the day. Promptly at 12:15 a musical soloist—a flautist, perhaps, or a pianist—would play a selection of classical music. Worshipers used this time to listen, think, and pray—the ideal preparation for hearing God's Word.

The musical prelude was followed by a warm welcome, a reading from Scripture, and a prayer for God's blessing on the city of Philadelphia. Then Dr. Boice or I would preach a 15-minute message, followed by a musical postlude that gave our listeners time to reflect on what they had heard. The whole service was over in half an hour, so that people could return on time.

For the first year of the Friday Lunch Easter Series, as we called it, Dr. Boice and I followed another venerable tradition and spoke on the seven "Last Words of Christ." In church tradition, these are the seven things that Jesus said during the hours that he suffered on the cross ("Father, forgive," "I thirst," "It is finished," and so forth).

The following year Dr. Boice and I preached on "The *Real* Last Words of Christ." These were things that Jesus said to His friends after He rose from the dead. Crucifixion was not the end for Jesus. Three days later, He came back to life and returned to His disciples. This means that the traditional "Last Words of Christ" were not His last words after all, but only the last words He spoke before rising again from the grave. So Dr. Boice and I preached on such important sayings such as "Touch me and see," "Feed my sheep," and "Go into all the world and preach the gospel"—things that Jesus said at the very end of the biblical gospels.

Then, in 1998, we took our preaching plan one step farther and gave a sermon series based on things that the New Testament said about the cross of Christ after Jesus ascended to heaven. In effect, these are the last words of the Father and the Spirit about the Son and His saving work. The texts we chose all had something to say about the crucifixion. Although Dr. Boice helped craft the series, he was traveling more that year and I did almost all the preaching. Those messages are published in this book, with an additional chapter on Philippians 2:8.

Our purpose in preaching these lunchtime messages was partly didactic: we wanted to explain the cross of Christ as clearly as we could. We also wanted to do this comprehensively, teaching the message of the crucifixion in all its fullness.

The messages in this book attempt to do the same thing by showing how multi-dimensional the cross is. There are seven chapters, exploring seven different implications of the crucifixion of Jesus Christ:

> its necessity for salvation;
>
> the offense it gives to Jews, Gentiles, and any moral individual;
>
> the peace it brings to those who trust in Christ;
>
> the power it has for achieving God's loving, saving purpose;
>
> the triumph it wins over sin, death, and the judgment of God;
>
> the humility it displays in the character of Jesus; and
>
> the boast it becomes for every believer.

But perhaps our primary purpose in preaching the cross was evangelistic: we wanted to explain the gospel as clearly as we could to people who did not have a saving relationship with Jesus Christ. So in addition to hoping that *Salvation by Crucifixion* will help you understand the cross of Christ in new and life-changing ways, I also hope that you will share it with a friend who does not know Jesus.

Introduction

This little book explains why the crucifixion of Jesus Christ is the most important event in human history.

Sometime during or near the year 33 A.D. Jesus of Nazareth was arrested, tried, condemned, and crucified. These events took place under the authority of Pontius Pilate, who served as Prefect of Judea under the Roman Emperor Tiberius. By Pilate's sentence, Jesus was taken outside Jerusalem, nailed to a wooden post, and left to die.

The significance of this brutal execution goes far beyond its immediate cultural context. The full meaning of the cross depends partly on the unique identity of Jesus Christ, whom the Bible presents *both* as a real human being *and* as the truly divine Son of God. Jesus is not merely a man, but at one and the same time also God—humanity and deity in a single person. This makes His death unprecedented: the crucifixion of Jesus Christ is the death of someone perfect and divine.

The implications of the crucifixion must also be understood in the context of the Old Testament. These sacred scriptures revealed that humanity had fallen into sin and thus had become alienated from God. Because the just penalty for sin was death, the only way to be forgiven and therefore reconciled to God was through offering sacrifices—specifically, bloody sacrifices of perfect animals. Yet there were prophecies that eventually a single sacrifice would atone for sin once and for all, as well as hints that this would be the sacrifice of a human being, not merely a bull, or sheep, or goat.

The death of Jesus on a cross—His execution by crucifixion—fulfilled the ancient promises by providing a permanent sacrifice for sin that reconciled humanity to God. There is forgiveness for anyone who places personal trust in Jesus Christ and His cross. This means something more than simply believing that Christ was crucified, which after all is an indisputable fact of history. Not only is the crucifixion plainly recorded in the biblical gospels, but it is also confirmed in the Jewish *Talmud*, the *Annals* of the Roman historian Tacitus, and elsewhere. Believing that Christ was crucified is not a religious commitment, therefore, but a simple recognition of a historical fact.

The meaning of the cross goes much further, however. The Bible teaches a message of salvation by crucifixion. In addition to standing as a culminating event in the life story of Jesus of Nazareth, the cross provided a perfect payment of the death penalty that sin deserves. We know that this payment was accepted by God because the crucifixion was followed by the resurrection—by Jesus coming back to everlasting life on the third day. This miracle proved that humanity was indeed reconciled to God and opened the only door to never-ending life, which God will give to anyone who has faith in Jesus.

If this is true, then it is the most important truth ever told. The crucifixion and resurrection of Jesus Christ give humanity hope that there is an answer to the fatal problem of death. But is this message true?

Why is it true? How can it be true? And if it is true, what difference does it make for my life? These are some of the questions that this little book hopes to answer.

1 The Necessity of the Cross

"This man was handed over to you by God's set purpose and foreknowledge."

ACTS 2:23

Christianity is all about the cross. By cross is meant the wooden post upon which Jesus of Nazareth was crucified. This was a standard means of execution in Roman times. Two wooden beams were nailed together in the shape of a cross or a T. The wrists and ankles of the victim were nailed to the wood, which was then slotted into the ground. There the man hung until he died.

The cross has always been the central symbol of Christianity. When archaeologists dig through the ruins of antiquity, they have one certain way to identify a place of Christian worship. They look for a cross. When they find it painted on a wall, carved into stone, or even worked into a floor plan, they know that they have found a church.

Since the beginning, Christians have identified themselves with the cross on which Jesus died. It is the chief symbol and defining reality of Christian faith.

NO LONGER NECESSARY?

Unfortunately, the cross is not as important as it used to be. At least, that is what leading thinkers are saying about the contemporary church. George Lindbeck, who taught theology at Yale, thinks that the cross has become a dead symbol: "A void has opened in the heart of Western Christianity. Where the cross once stood is now a vacuum."[1]

Not that the cross has disappeared altogether, of course. Not yet, anyway. It still stands atop church steeples. It appears on church letterheads. It is stamped into Bible covers and even breath-mints at the local Christian bookstore. It dangles from postmodern ears. Yet, the cross of Christ is no longer a living reality for the people of God.

---

1. George Lindbeck, "Justification and Atonement: An Ecumenical Trajectory," unpublished paper, pp. 45-46.

At an infamous theology conference in the early 1990s, one speaker objected to Christianity's seeming obsession with the cross. "I don't think we need folks hanging on crosses and blood dripping and weird stuff," the speaker said. In other words, who needs the cross?

It is true that there is something unsightly, even grotesque, about crucifixion. The Bible does not overlook this horror. Concerning Jesus, the prophet Isaiah said, "Like one from whom men hide their faces he was despised" (Isa. 53:3). The cross is as unsightly as it is unpopular. But it is still necessary. Wherever the cross disappears, true religion disappears, for there is no Christianity without the cross.

NECESSARY TO FULFILL GOD'S PLAN

Why is the cross of Christ essential to Christianity? For several reasons. First, the cross was necessary to fulfill God's eternal plan.

There was a time when Jesus Himself wondered if the cross was truly necessary. It was the night He went to pray in the Garden of Gethsemane. He knew that His enemies were closing in on Him. In fact, later the same night He would be betrayed, arrested, and sentenced to death.

Jesus knew that the end was near. Like any human being, He was horrified by the prospect of death. Although Jesus is God, He is also a human being. As a human being, He wondered if it was necessary for Him to die such a painful death. Considering what it would be like to be crucified, He said, "'My soul is overwhelmed with sorrow to the point of death.' Going a little farther, he fell with his face to the ground and prayed, 'My Father, if it is possible, may this cup be taken from me'" (Matt. 26:38-39). Jesus was asking His Father if there was any way He could save His people without being crucified.

Yet because it was an essential part of His plan, God the Father did not spare God the Son from the cross. Jesus explained this after He was crucified and had come back to life. He spoke with two of His disciples, who were puzzled by what had happened to Him. They did not understand why Jesus died on a cross. He answered, "Did not the Christ have to suffer these things?" (Luke 24:26). According to God's eternal plan, the cross of Christ was inevitable.

Christians, therefore, have always believed and taught the necessity of the cross. Not long after Jesus returned to heaven, His friend Peter preached to the people of Jerusalem. He said: "This man [Jesus] was handed over to you by God's set purpose and foreknowledge; and you, with the help of wicked men, put him to death by nailing him to the cross" (Acts 2:23). God knew about the crucifixion of His Son even before it happened. He not only knew about it, but He also permitted it. He not only permitted it, but He also purposed it. The cross was essential to His plan for humanity.

This is worth remembering whenever it seems as if God doesn't know what He is doing. The trials and tragedies of life are often puzzling. Does God know what is happening in my life? Does He care? Can He do anything about it? The answer is that God does know and does care. And if you trust Him, He will do something about it.

The cross of Christ proves that God's plans are good. The crucifixion of Jesus Christ was the most evil deed ever committed on this planet. God's own perfect Son was put to death by wicked men. What could be more evil than that? At the same time, however, the crucifixion of Jesus was the best thing that ever happened on this planet. As we shall see, the cross has brought salvation to the world. If God brought the greatest good out of the greatest evil, then He can bring good out of what seems to be evil in our own lives. It is all part of God's good plan.

NECESSARY TO PAY FOR SIN

What made crucifixion part of God's plan in the first place? Why was the cross necessary? What was it necessary for?

The cross was part of God's plan because it was the only way to save human beings from their sins. In the words of John Owen (1616-1683), the great Puritan and Oxford theologian, "There is no death of sin without the death of Christ."[2] Understanding sin, therefore, is part of understanding the cross.

What *is* sin? The answer is twofold. Sin is: (1) doing anything God forbids, or (2) failing to do anything God requires.

First, sin means doing what God forbids, as stipulated in Scripture. Whenever we curse God, tell a small untruth, steal office supplies, or strike out at someone in anger, we commit a sin. We have broken God's commandment against cursing, lying, stealing, or murder.

---

2. See John Owen's profound work *The Death of Death in the Death of Christ* (Edinburgh: Banner of Truth, 1959).

Second, sin also includes not doing what the Word of God requires. God wants people to worship Him, to put others before themselves, to care for the sick and give to the poor. With these requirements it is worth asking, "What have I done for God lately?" If the answer is "Not very much," then we are sinning by not doing what God requires.

The reason sin is a problem is because God is holy. God is so perfectly holy that it is impossible for any sinful human being to stand before Him. Sin brings us under divine judgment. We deserve to be cursed and damned for our sins.

This is why Christ's death on the cross was such a necessary part of God's plan. God wanted to save His people from their sins. But how could He deal with this sin without sacrificing either His love or His holiness? This was the problem.

God could not simply overlook our sins. This might have been loving, but it would not have been holy. Justice would not have been served. Our sins would not have been paid for. Nor did God simply condemn us to die for our own sins, which would have been holy, but would not have fully demonstrated God's love.

The place where God's love and God's holiness embrace is at the cross. God the Father sent His Son, His only Son, to suffer and to die for our sins. His life for our life, His pain for our gain: here is the love of God. And here also, in the cross, is the holiness of God. The death penalty is executed against sin. The sins of God's people are paid in full.

The cross of Christ is necessary to preserve both God's love and God's holiness in the salvation of God's people. The German theologian Emil Brunner (1889–1966) explained that the cross of Christ "is the event in which God makes known his holiness and his love simultaneously, in one event, in an absolute manner. ... The cross is the only place where the loving, forgiving, merciful God is revealed in such a way that we perceive that his holiness and his love are equally infinite."[3]

Necessary to Save

There is one other way in which the cross is necessary. The cross is essential for our salvation. Anyone who wants to go to heaven must first go to the cross. Eternal life is God's

---

3.   Emil Brunner, *The Mediator*, trans. Olive Wyon (1927; reprint, Philadelphia: Westminster, 1947), pp. 450, 470.

free gift for anyone who believes that Jesus died for his or her sins on the cross.

To begin with, this means believing that the crucifixion really happened. The historical records show that Jesus of Nazareth was crucified by Roman soldiers on a hill just outside Jerusalem in A.D. 30 Believing in Jesus' death on the cross means believing that if you had been there that day, you could have touched His cross and received a splinter in your finger—that's how real it was. The Christ on the cross was a living, bleeding, dying person. To become a believer is to accept that Jesus Christ lived a real life and died a real death.

But believing Jesus died on the cross also means something more. It means believing that He did what He did for your salvation. It means acknowledging that you, personally, are a sinner. It means confessing that you need Jesus Christ to save you from the wrath and curse of God. It means believing that Jesus died on that splintery old cross for your own personal sins. To become a believer is to accept that Jesus Christ is not merely a legend; He lived a real life and died a real death.

Understanding that Jesus died, or even that He died for sinners, is only part of the faith that God requires. For example, one woman decided to become a member of the church she was attending. So she went to be interviewed by the church elders. They asked her what she thought it meant to be a Christian. Among other things, she explained how Jesus died on the cross to pay for sin.

The woman's theology was sound, but the elders still felt a little uneasy about the woman's testimony. They were not sure she was a genuine Christian. This was because she spoke in a casual way, as if the cross had little relevance to her own life. There are plenty of people like her in the church. They consider themselves Christians, but they have not made a personal life-and-death commitment to Jesus Christ.

So the elders asked her a follow-up question: "Do you believe that Jesus died on the cross, not just for the sins of others, but for your sins?" There was a long pause, and finally the woman said, "I've never thought about it that way before."

The elders explained to her that she needed to confess that she herself was one of the sinners for whom Christ died. That night she believed that Jesus died on the cross for her sins and received Him as her personal Savior.

This woman came to understand what everyone must understand to be saved: the necessity of the cross. The cross is necessary, not just in a general way as part of God's eternal plan, but necessary for your very own salvation from sin and death.

2 The Offense of the Cross

"... who for the joy set before him endured the cross, scorning its shame."

HEBREWS 12:2

The cross has become so familiar that it has lost its power to offend. It is no longer offensive to Christians because they are used to seeing it, talking about it, hearing about it, and singing about it all the time. Nor is the cross offensive to non-Christians. For them it is a symbol of religious commitment, or perhaps a fashion accessory. For many, the cross of Christ has been tamed.

The taming of the cross is a sign that its true meaning has been lost. For as soon as people understand what crucifixion means, the cross becomes completely offensive to them. The early Christian theologian Origen

(c. 185-c. 254) rightly called it the "utterly vile death of the cross."[1]

AN ABOMINATION TO THE ROMANS

The cross was an abomination to the Romans: a brutal means of execution. It was the electric chair or the lethal injection of the ancient world, and the end of death row is no place for sentimentality. There is nothing pretty about an execution.

Not only was crucifixion a means of execution, but it was also the most gruesome means imaginable. Marcus Tullius Cicero (B.C. 106-43) described it as "a most cruel and disgusting punishment."[2] The cross was associated with torture, bleeding, nakedness, and agony. It was designed to kill only after the victim had endured the maximum possible suffering.

Not surprisingly, crucifixion was meant for criminals, and only for hardened criminals at that. The great New Testament scholar F. F. Bruce wrote, "To die by crucifixion was to plumb the lowest

---

1.   Origen, Commentary on Matthew 27:22ff., quoted in F. F. Bruce, *The Epistle to the Hebrews*, New International Commentary on the New Testament (Grand Rapids, MI: Eerdmans, 1990), p. 338.

2.   Cicero, *In Verrem*, II, 5, 165, quoted in John Stott, *The Cross of Christ* (Downers Grove, IL: InterVarsity, 1986), p. 24.

depths of disgrace; it was a punishment reserved for those who were deemed most unfit to live, a punishment for those who were subhuman."[3] The cross was for murderers and rebels, provided they were also slaves or foreigners.

All of these reasons explain why the cross was an offense to the Romans, so much so that they refused to allow their own citizens to be crucified, no matter what they had done. Cicero claimed, "It is a crime to put a Roman citizen in chains, it is an enormity to flog one, sheer murder to slay one; what, then, shall I say of crucifixion? It is impossible to find the word for such an abomination."[4]

Indeed, there was no word for it. No polite word, at any rate, for the word for *cross* was taboo in Roman society. To quote again from Cicero, "Let the very mention of the cross be far removed not only from a Roman citizen's body, but from his mind, his eyes, his ears."[5] *Crux* was a Latin swear word.

Since the Romans considered crucifixion an abomination, it is not surprising that many of them held Christianity in derision. A fascinating example comes from the Palatine Hill in

3. Bruce, p. 338.
4. Cicero, *In Verrem*, II, 5, 170, quoted in Stott, p. 24.
5. Cicero, *Pro Rabirio*, 16, quoted in Bruce, p. 338.

Rome. There, on the wall of a house, the oldest surviving picture of the crucifixion was found, in the form of graffiti. The crude drawing depicts a man with a head of a donkey stretched on a cross. Another man stands at the foot of the cross with one arm raised in worship. A taunt is scribbled underneath: "Alexamenos worships God."[6] Thus the Romans poured their scorn on those who worshiped a crucified man.

A CURSE TO THE JEWS

As offensive as crucifixion was to the Romans, it was even more offensive to the Jews. According to Hebrew law, any man who was crucified was under a divine curse. The Torah said: "If a man guilty of a capital offense is put to death and his body is hung on a tree, you must not leave his body on the tree overnight. Be sure to bury him that same day, because anyone who is hung on a tree is under God's curse" (Deut. 21:22-23).

The curse of the cross explains why Jesus was crucified outside Jerusalem. Crucifixion was such an abomination that the Jews never would have allowed it to take place within the sacred precincts of their holy city. The cursed death of the cursed man had to take place outside the city wall.

---

6.   Stott, p. 25.

The biblical curse also explains something curious about the way the first Christians described the cross. They often referred to it as a "tree." For example, when the apostle Peter preached to the leaders of Jerusalem, he said, "The God of our fathers raised Jesus from the dead—whom you had killed by hanging him on a tree" (Acts 5:30). He said the same thing when he traveled to Caesarea and spoke to a Roman soldier named Cornelius: "We are witnesses of everything [Jesus] did in the country of the Jews and in Jerusalem. They killed him by hanging him on a tree" (Acts 10:39).

The apostle Paul described the crucifixion in the same way. He went to the synagogue in Pisidian Antioch and testified, "The people of Jerusalem and their rulers did not recognize Jesus, yet in condemning him they fulfilled the words of the prophets that are read every Sabbath. Though they found no proper ground for a death sentence, they asked Pilate to have him executed. When they had carried out all that was written about him, they took him down from the tree and laid him in a tomb" (Acts 13:27-29).

What is curious about these statements is that they speak of a "tree" rather than a "cross." Both terms are appropriate, but calling the cross a "tree" serves as a reminder of the Old Testament curse.

Because of that curse one might even say that the cross was an offense to God the Father, for He was the one who had cursed the cross in the first place. It was His Word that stated that anyone hung upon a tree was accursed. God's Son Jesus Christ experienced that curse when He was crucified. Shortly before His death the sky turned black, and "Jesus cried out in a loud voice, *'Eloi, Eloi, lama sabachthani?'*—which means, 'My God, my God, why have you forsaken me?'" (Matt. 27:46). Jesus died a God-forsaken death on a God-forsaken cross.

Why did the first Christians call attention to the fact that Jesus died on a tree? The very idea is offensive to the Jewish ear. In fact, in an ancient literary dialogue between Justin the Christian and Trypho the Jew, Trypho refused to believe that God's Messiah possibly could have died upon a tree: "But whether Christ should be so shamefully crucified, this we are in doubt about. For whosoever is crucified is said in the law to be accursed, so that I am exceedingly incredulous on this point."[7]

7. Justin Martyr, *Dialogue with Trypho, a Jew*, ch. 89, eds. Alexander Roberts and James Donaldson, *Ante-Nicene Fathers* (New York, 1885; reprint, Peabody, MA: Hendrickson, 1994), 1:244.

Yet the first Christians were not ashamed to let everyone know that Jesus died on a cursed cross. They understood that by being crucified, He had taken God's curse against their sin upon Himself. The apostle Peter put it like this: "He himself bore our sins in his body on the tree" (1 Pet. 2:24). The reason Jesus died an accursed death on the cross was to undergo the curse we deserve for our sin.

The offense of the cross went all the way back to the Old Testament curse of the tree. The apostle Paul made this connection explicit when he wrote: "Christ redeemed us from the curse of the law by becoming a curse for us, for it is written: 'Cursed is everyone who is hung on a tree'" (Gal. 3:13).

AN AFFRONT TO EVERY MORAL INDIVIDUAL

The cross was an abomination to the Romans and a curse to the Jews. And to this day it remains offensive to anyone who thinks he or she is a good person.

Most people have a rather high opinion of themselves. They are impressed with their own moral record. They generally tell the truth. They usually put in an honest day's work. They are always kind to animals. True, they may have a few minor flaws, but by and large they are good people. Their virtues far outweigh their vices. Certainly they are good enough to get into heaven. They are not saints, perhaps, but one way or another they will be able to squeeze through the pearly gates.

The cross offends the sensibilities of moral people by utterly contradicting this line of reasoning. Consider what the cross says. It says that we are *unrighteous*. It says that we are sinners. It says that we do not measure up to God's perfect standard. The reason it was necessary for Jesus to be crucified was because of the sins of humanity, our own sins included.

The cross also says that we are *helpless*. It says that we cannot get into heaven on the strength of our own record. We need someone else to offer his perfect life on our behalf. This is one difference between Christianity and every other religion. Every other religion tells us to present to God the best record we can. Christianity teaches instead that God offers His perfect record to us. But this means that we cannot gain eternal life without His total help. The death of Christ on the cross proves the helplessness of humanity.

Then the cross says we are *hopeless*. The cross of Christ shows that sin deserves the wrath and curse of God. It proves that without Christ, sinners will perish for their sins. Surely if God could have saved us any other way, He would have done it. But there was no other way, because every sin deserves a hell of suffering.

Who wants to be told that he or she is hopeless, helpless, and unrighteous? No one! The very idea is offensive. Most people are convinced of their own basic goodness. They go through life helping themselves and hoping for the best. These attitudes make the cross offensive to the moral individual. The cross is a warning that we are dead in our sins. It announces that we cannot help ourselves, indeed, that without Christ we are without hope.

JESUS SCORNED THE CROSS

We are hopeless, helpless, and unrighteous—unless we come to the cross to ask for the hope, the help, and the righteousness of Jesus Christ. Then we find that the cross is full of the hope and the help we need.

Jesus is the one person who did not find the cross offensive. He was not disgraced by its disgrace. So the Bible encourages us to "fix our eyes on Jesus ... who ... endured the cross, scorning its shame, and sat down at the right hand of the throne of God" (Heb. 12:2).

Jesus scorned the shame of the cross. He had heard that it was an abomination to the Romans. He knew that it was a curse to the Jews, and even to God the Father. He recognized that it was an affront to everyone who wants to get to heaven on his or her own merits. Yet, however offensive the cross may be to others, Jesus Christ scorned its shame and allowed it to fall upon Himself for our eternal benefit, not allowing that shame to make Him turn back from atoning for our sins.

Christ's scorn for the shame of the cross explains the remarkable fact that the cross has survived at all. How could such an offensive emblem persist through the centuries? How could a symbol that was scorned by the Romans, cursed by the Jews, and dismissed by every moral individual endure from one millennium to the next?

Only because the cross was no offense to Jesus Christ. For Him, it was the price He gladly paid to save His people. And for everyone who loves Him, the cross ceases to be an offense. It becomes instead the proof of the undying love of the Savior who gave His life for us.

3 ⌜The Peace of the Cross⌟

*"... making peace through his blood,
shed on the cross."*

COLOSSIANS 1:20

It is not easy to make peace on earth, and once peace has been made, it is even harder to keep. Neville Chamberlain (1869-1940) learned these lessons the hard way at the outset of World War II. In September 1938, when Chamberlain served as Prime Minister of Britain, he signed the Munich Agreement with Adolf Hitler. Upon his return to Britain, he proudly announced that he had achieved "peace in our time."

Twelve months later Hitler invaded Poland, and the world was pulled into the abyss of war. Neville Chamberlain proved to be a prophet like those Jeremiah warned about in the Old

Testament: "'Peace, peace,' they say, when there is no peace" (Jer. 8:11).

Rumors of peace continue to be whispered at the present time. From time to time peace is announced in the Balkans, Northern Ireland, the Middle East, or elsewhere. World leaders sign their treaties. The media gather. The crowds cheer. Yet there is no peace. In fact, politicians no longer speak of "peace," but only of a "peace process." As far as anyone can tell, it is all process and very little peace.

At War with God

There is a reason why the world seems always to be at war. It is because humanity is in rebellion against God. Ever since the day when Adam and Eve ate the forbidden fruit, there has been an unceasing war between God and the people He made. The hostilities began with the sin of our first parents, and soon escalated:

> Then the eyes of both of them were opened, and they realized they were naked; so they sewed fig leaves together and made coverings for themselves. Then the man and his wife heard the sound of the Lord God as he was walking in the garden in the cool of the day, and they hid from the Lord God among the trees of the garden. But the Lord God called to the man, "Where are

you?" He answered, "I heard you in the garden, and I was afraid because I was naked; so I hid." (Gen. 3:7-10)

Camouflage and retreat—these are the stratagems of war! Adam and Eve knew that a breach had come between themselves and God. The sound of God's footstep, which once they had greeted with joy, now filled them with dread. By trying to cover up and hide, our first parents were drawing the battle lines.

Every human being is a son of Adam or a daughter of Eve. Therefore, everyone enters this world already at war with God. This is true of any child born in wartime. The child's allegiance already has been determined. He or she has chosen sides, or rather, had them chosen. In the same way, every human born into this world is prepared to take up arms against God.

How can we tell that we are at war with God? First, there is the testimony of God's Word, which says we are "alienated from God and enemies in [our] minds because of [our] evil behavior" (Col. 1:21). We love everything the world has to offer, but "friendship with the world is hatred toward God" (James 4:4). We know we are "God's enemies " because the Bible tells us so (Rom. 5:10).

Then there is the evidence of a troubled conscience. Do you ever feel guilty for something you think, say, or do? Do you ever get angry unjustly? Do you ever say anything untrue? Do you ever take anything that does not belong to you? Most people have guilty consciences. There are times when they would rather not have God know where they have been, what they have been doing, or what they have been thinking. The guilty conscience is an alarm of war. It testifies that our sin has made us enemies of God.

Another way to tell that we do not have peace with God is that we are not at peace with one another. Divorce is on the rise. Child abuse is rampant. The legal system is overwhelmed with a backlog of lawsuits and countersuits. To say nothing of long-standing feuds between neighbors or petty gossip in the workplace. If we were at peace with God, there would be peace in our times. But as it is, the whole world is at war.

A PEACE-OFFERING

What the world needs is the peace of the cross. The place where our war against heaven comes to an end is at the cross of Christ: "God was pleased ... through [Jesus] to reconcile to himself all things ... by making peace through his blood, shed on the cross" (Col. 1:19-20).

One of the terms the Bible uses to describe peace between God and humanity is *reconciliation*. The basic meaning of *reconcile* is to make an exchange.[1] The word was used in biblical times to describe making change in the marketplace. Suppose that you hand me a dollar bill. If I give you back two quarters, two dimes, five nickels, and five pennies, we have been reconciled. We have made a fair transaction (trust me!).

When the Bible speaks about reconciliation with God, it means that an exchange has taken place. There is a change in our relationship with him. Hatred has been traded in for love. We are no longer God's enemies; now we are His friends.

Reconciliation does not mean that we simply change our minds about God. Left to ourselves, we never would change our minds about God. We would continue in perpetual rebellion. Reconciliation never would take place. If men and women are to be reconciled to God, God must take the first step. He has to take the initiative. And He does.

---

1. Leon Morris, *The Apostolic Preaching of the Cross* (London, 1965; reprint, Grand Rapids, MI: Eerdmans, 1994), p. 215.

Leon Morris explains that "God is never said in so many words to be reconciled to man. Almost always he is the subject of the verb and is said to reconcile man to Himself. This manner of speaking puts emphasis on the truth that the process of reconciliation originates with God. It is only by the out-working of his love that man can be brought into right relationships with his Maker."[2] Thus, whenever the Bible speaks about reconciliation, God is always the one who does the reconciling. Colossians 1 is a good example: "God was ... pleased to reconcile to himself all things" (vv. 19-20).

Reconciliation teaches something remarkable about the character of God, namely, that He befriends His enemies. God loves those who hate Him. He offers peace to those who have waged war against Him. Although He is the one who has been wronged, He is the one who makes things right. And He does all this while the battle still rages: "When we were God's enemies, we were reconciled to him through the death of his Son" (Rom. 5:10).

The way God reconciles us to Himself is through the cross of Christ; specifically,

---

2.   Ibid., p. 220.

through the blood of Christ. God made "peace through his blood, shed on the cross" (Col. 1:20). The crucifixion of Jesus Christ was a peace-offering. The breach between humanity and God was caused by sin. Our sin had to be paid for and removed in order for reconciliation to take place.

Peace never occurs simply by ignoring what started the war in the first place. True reconciliation depends on dealing with the real problem. H. Maldwyn Hughes explains that "there can be no reconciliation between persons by ignoring the deep-seated ground of offence. This must be eradicated and destroyed if the reconciliation is to be complete and lasting. If God and man are to be reconciled, it cannot be by the simple expedient of ignoring sin, but only by overcoming it."[3]

This is one of the things that Jesus was doing on the cross. He was atoning for, defeating, and overcoming sin so that we could be reconciled to God. The prophet Isaiah put this in a beautiful way: "the punishment that brought us peace was upon him" (Isa. 53:5).

It is striking that when the Bible speaks about the peace of the cross, it uses the past

---

3. H. Maldwyn Hughes, *What Is the Atonement?* (London: J. Clarke & Co. Ltd, 1924), p. 146.

tense. In one way or another, Scripture says that Jesus Christ has already reconciled man to God on the cross. This is because the crucifixion is an historical event. Therefore, the reconciliation between God and humanity is complete. According to the Scottish theologian P. T. Forsyth, "Reconciliation was finished in Christ's death. Paul did not preach a gradual reconciliation. He preached what the old divines used to call the finished work.... He preached something done once for all."[4]

Reconciliation has already been accomplished! Yet the peace of the cross still needs to be received. A sinner is not reconciled to God until he or she actually goes to the cross to be reconciled. It is only by trusting in the finished work of Christ that anyone finds peace with God.

BLESSED ARE THE PEACEMAKERS

Peace with God is not the end of the story, however. Everyone who has peace with God also must live at peace with other people. "God ... reconciled us to himself through Christ and gave us the ministry of reconciliation: that

---

4.   P. T. Forsyth, *The Work of Christ* (London: Fontana, 1948), p. 86.

God was reconciling the world to himself in Christ, not counting men's sins against them. And he has committed to us the message of reconciliation" (2 Cor. 5:18-19).

In other words, having peace with God means living at peace with everyone else. Christians must have peaceful relationships with their families, friends, neighbors, and co-workers. Anyone who has an enemy must do what God did for His enemies, namely, take the initiative to make reconciliation. This is not always possible, but the Bible tells Christians to "make every effort to live in peace with all men" (Heb. 12:14). One sign that we are at peace with God is that we seek to make peace with one another.

Once there were two women who were not at peace. They had attended the same church for many years. In fact, they had been the best of friends. Yet one of the women had committed a serious offense against the other. As a result of her malice, the other woman was driven away from the church. A close friendship degenerated into bitter animosity. For years they neither saw nor spoke to one another.

Then one day they were reconciled. It happened in the dairy section at the supermarket. The woman who had been wronged bent over to pick up a carton of milk. When she stood up, her adversary was there, with her arms open wide. As they embraced, she apologized for what she had done, and they were reconciled.

The peace between the two women flowed from the peace of the cross. Their reconciliation was one small part of what the Bible means when it says, "God was pleased to have all his fullness dwell in [Jesus], and through him to reconcile to himself all things, whether things on earth or things in heaven, by making peace through his blood, shed on the cross" (Col. 1:19-20). If we have experienced this peace through the reconciling work of Jesus Christ, then we will seek peace with one another.

4 The Power of the Cross

"The message of the cross is foolishness to those who are perishing, but to us who are being saved it is the power of God."

I CORINTHIANS 1:18

It is hard to imagine anything weaker than a man hanging on a cross. Since he is naked, he is completely vulnerable. He is exposed not only to the elements, but also to the shame of his nakedness. His body is there for all to see in all its frailty.

The weakness of the cross is also physical. The longer the man hangs on the cross, the weaker he becomes. His heart and breath grow faint until he expires. There is nothing he can do to save himself from his inevitable demise. A man crucified is a weakling. He is a victim, not a victor.

The weakness of a crucified man may help to explain why so many people have rejected

Jesus Christ. Perhaps they have heard about His teaching. They know that His biography is contained somewhere in the Bible. They may even believe that He was crucified. But it does not seem to matter. What is so significant about a man hanging on a cross?

THE OLD, FOOLISH CROSS

Christians believe that the crucifixion of Jesus Christ, with His resurrection, was the most important event in the history of the world. For them, the cross of Christ is the source of all hope and comfort. Yet the same cross that is so attractive to the followers of Christ is exactly what keeps others from coming to Him at all.

This was true already in the time of Christ. The Jews were looking for something supernatural. Under Roman occupation, they controlled neither their economy nor their destiny. So the Jews "demand[ed] miraculous signs" (1 Cor. 1:22). They expected God to send a king to deliver them from Roman oppression. They were looking for a supernatural deliverance by a mighty warrior. They would not believe in Jesus unless He showed them a miraculous sign.

The Greeks were looking for proof of a different kind. They were the intellectuals of the ancient world. They spent their time talking about nothing except "the latest ideas" (Acts 17:21). When it came to religion, the Greeks were rationalists. They would not believe that Jesus was the Savior of the world until someone proved it to them on the basis of reasoned evidence. The "Greeks look[ed] for wisdom" (1 Cor. 1:22).

These attitudes explain why neither the Jews nor the Greeks had very much interest in Jesus Christ. He was simply a man hanging on a cross. Christ crucified was an obstacle to the Jews. The Bible calls the crucifixion "a stumbling block" (v. 23) that prevented many of them from coming to salvation. What is so miraculous about a man executed like a common criminal? To the Jews, the cross was an obstacle because it was weak.

To the Greeks, the cross was not so much an obstacle as it was foolishness. Where is the wisdom in dying a God-forsaken death? How could the blood of one man atone for the sins of the whole world? The cross was unimpressive to the Greeks because it did not appeal to their superior intellect. Therefore, Christ crucified was "foolishness to Gentiles" (v. 23) as well as "a stumbling block" to Jews.

The cross of Christ remains an obstacle to the modern mind. Many religious people are looking for exactly what people were looking for in the time of Christ. They will not trust in Jesus until God shows them another miracle or gives them better proof.

Like the ancient Jews, some are waiting for a supernatural sign. This explains the popularity of fortune-tellers and faith healers. For a small fee they will reveal the future or perform a televised miracle. When it comes to Christianity, some people demand a miracle before they will believe in Jesus Christ. "If only God would come down out of heaven and show himself to me, then I would believe him," they say.

Miracle-seekers are like the boy in a short story by John Updike called *Pigeon Feathers*: "Though the experiment frightened him, he lifted his hands high into the darkness above his face and begged Christ to touch them. Not hard or long: the faintest, quickest grip would be final for a lifetime."[1] Eventually, God did touch the boy—but not with physical hands.

Other people are looking for wisdom. Not many perhaps, but at least some. They go to the university. They study philosophy. They

---

1. John Updike, *Pigeon Feathers and Other Stories* (New York: Fawcett Crest, 1963), p. 92.

read about the latest advances in human science. When it comes to religion, they want God to answer all their questions. They refuse to believe in Jesus Christ until someone can unravel the mysteries of nature, or solve the problem of human freedom, or show them physical evidence for the existence of the soul. They are like the philosopher Bertrand Russell (1872-1970), who once explained to an interviewer what he would say if suddenly he found himself in heaven and saw God before his very eyes: "Sir, why did you not give me better evidence?"[2]

The world is still looking for a proof of mind or miracle. But all Christianity offers is a God-man dying on a cross. Crucifixion does not even show up on the radar of postmodern expectations. If God wants to perform some other miracle or provide some other proof, then perhaps the world will listen. But until such time, the old, foolish cross remains an obstacle to faith.

THE POWER OF LOVE

The cross of Christ refuses to meet human expectations. At one level the crucifixion

---

2. Sir Bertrand Russell, quoted in Leo Rosten, "Bertrand Russell and God: A Memoir," *The Saturday Review* (February 23, 1974), p. 26.

of Jesus is just another Roman execution. It seems weak to those who look for strength. It appears foolish to those who look for wisdom. But this is only when the cross is viewed in human terms.

From God's perspective, the cross is neither impotent nor ignorant, but full of power and wisdom: "The message of the cross is foolishness to those who are perishing, but to us who are being saved it is the power of God" (1 Cor. 1:18). To understand this, it helps to remember that God is much wiser and stronger than any human being. God has more intelligence than all the geniuses in the world put together. He has more power in His left pinky, so to speak, than the world's strongest man has in his entire biceps. To quote again from the Bible, "the foolishness of God is wiser than man's wisdom, and the weakness of God is stronger than man's strength" (v. 25).

However weak or foolish it may seem to mere mortals, the cross of Christ displays the power and wisdom of God. It does this in several ways. First, it is a powerful demonstration of God's love.

When it comes to love, actions speak louder than words. A man may say that he loves a woman, but how can she know for sure? She will know that he really does love her when he shows her his love. A gift would be nice, especially if the gift is precious or rare. Or if the gift comes at great cost. Or best of all, if the gift is what she has always needed or wanted.

This is exactly the kind of gift that God gave when He sent Jesus to die on the cross. It was a precious gift because it was the gift of God's own Son. It was a rare gift because Jesus is God's only Son. It was a costly gift, the costliest of all, because it came at the expense of Jesus' lifeblood. Best of all, the cross of Christ was exactly the gift that humanity was hoping for. Jesus died on the cross to effect eternal friendship with God, which is the longing of every human heart: "For God so loved the world that he gave his one and only Son, that whoever believes in him shall not perish but have eternal life" (John 3:16).

The power of the cross is the power of love. When Jesus was crucified, he showed the full extent of God's love. For those who are looking for proof, the cross is proof enough. The crucifixion of Jesus Christ is the only evidence needed to demonstrate God's undying love for sinners.

THE WISDOM OF FORGIVENESS

The cross is also a powerful demonstration of God's wisdom—the wisdom of His forgiveness. Human beings do not approach God on an even footing. We come to Him having already accumulated an enormous debt, the debt we owe to God because of our sin. All the lies we have told, all the curses we have uttered, all the wounds we have inflicted, and all the worship we have withheld amount to an enormous debt of sin. How could such a vast debt ever be settled?

This is where God's wisdom comes in. God did not set up an elaborate payment plan that would take an eternity for sinners to pay off. Rather, the entire debt was settled on the cross. God accepted the sacrificial death of His Son as the full payment for sin. Jesus paid for each and every last sin when He was crucified. He died on the cross so that God could forgive all the sins of all His people all at once.

There is immense wisdom in the cross, therefore, as well as unlimited power. The wisdom and power of the cross are the wisdom and power of sin forgiven. For those who are looking for a miracle, the cross is miracle enough. The crucifixion of Jesus Christ offers full and free forgiveness.

POWER UNTO SALVATION

What do you think of the cross of Christ? Is it wise or foolish? Is it strong or weak? These questions demand an answer. The cross is either one or the other; it cannot be both. If the cross of Christ is the power of God unto salvation, then it is the strongest, wisest thing God has ever done. But if the cross has no power to save, then it is irrelevant to modern life. So the question bears repeating: What do you think of the cross of Christ?

Sadly, some people do not understand the cross, and some of them never will. The crucifixion of Jesus Christ will remain foolish to them until the day of judgment. This is because the cross only makes sense to those who are saved by it: "For the message of the cross is foolishness to those who are perishing, but to us who are being saved it is the power of God" (1 Cor. 1:18). To put this another way, the cross only makes sense to those who trust in Jesus Christ for their salvation. For them, the cross is the proof of God's love and the miracle of God's forgiveness. It is neither weak nor foolish, but strong and wise.

What should someone do if the cross still seems foolish? The obvious thing to do is to keep trying to understand it, asking God what it means. To anyone who asks for help instead of a miracle or proof, Jesus Christ gives the love and the forgiveness of the cross, which is the power of God.

5 The Triumph of the Cross

*"... having disarmed the powers and authorities, he
made a public spectacle of them, triumphing over
them by the cross."*

COLOSSIANS 2:15

When Jesus Christ was crucified outside
Jerusalem, at least three things were nailed
to His cross. The first was Jesus Himself. As
the Bible simply states, "They crucified him"
(Mark 15:24).

The Roman custom was to drive heavy
iron nails through the wrists and ankles of
the victim. This is what the Roman soldiers
did to Jesus: they "put him to death by nailing
him to the cross" (Acts 2:23). After He was
raised from the dead, Jesus was able to show
His disciples the nail prints in His hands
(John 20:25-27), because He had been nailed
to the cross.

Something else was nailed to the cross where Jesus died as well. It was the announcement the governor had "prepared and fastened to the cross. It read: 'JESUS OF NAZARETH, THE KING OF THE JEWS'" (John 19:19). This publicity was God's doing. He wanted everyone who witnessed the crucifixion to know that His Son was the true king of Israel. And in all likelihood that public notice was fastened to the cross of Christ with a hammer and a nail.

A CERTIFICATE OF DEBT

One more thing was nailed to the cross of Christ. Surprisingly, it was something God nailed to the cross Himself, even though it was invisible to the human eye. The Bible says that God "forgave us all our sins, having canceled the written code, with its regulations, that was against us and that stood opposed to us; he took it away, nailing it to the cross" (Col. 2:13-14). The third thing nailed to the cross was a "written code."

What kind of "written code" was it? To answer this question, it helps to know something about business transactions in the Roman world. The Greek word for "written code" (*cheirographon*) means "handwritten" or "signed by hand." It was used to refer to any kind of personal autograph.

The word also had a specialized meaning, however. In the world of finance it referred to a certificate of debt signed by the debtor's own hand. The famous Bible scholar J. B. Lightfoot (1828-1889) called it "a note of hand, a bond or obligation."[1] Today it might be called an I.O.U. A man who owed money carefully wrote out the amount he was obliged to pay back to his creditors. Then he confirmed the grand total of his indebtedness with his personal signature.

This gives us at least the beginning of an answer to our question. The "written code" God nailed to the cross was a bill of debt. But this raises still more questions. How large was the debt? To whom was it owed? Most important of all, whose autograph was at the bottom of the note?

The Bible gives enough clues to help us answer these questions. What was nailed to the cross was "the written code, with its regulations, that was against us and that stood opposed to us" (Col. 2:14). "Regulations" obviously has something to do with law. It calls to mind the rules for life that God first

---

1. J. B. Lightfoot, *St. Paul's Epistles to the Colossians and to Philemon* (London, 1875; reprint, Lynn, MA: Hendrickson, 1981), p. 187.

gave to Moses which are summarized in the Ten Commandments: "You shall have no other gods before me.... You shall not murder. You shall not commit adultery. You shall not steal," and so forth (Exod. 20:1-17).

There is nothing wrong with these regulations, which are perfectly righteous. God has every right to expect people to live good and holy lives. He has given us His rules for our good. Any society that worships God alone, safeguards life, preserves sex for marriage, and respects private property is a good society. God's law is not the problem, therefore.

The problem is that human beings are lawbreakers. According to the *Westminster Shorter Catechism*, "No mere man since the fall is able in this life perfectly to keep the commandments of God, but doth daily break them in thought, word, and deed" (Answer 82). We worship anything and everything except God. We curse God when things go wrong at the office. We do not give our fathers and mothers the respect they deserve. We lie, cheat, and steal. We are discontent with what we have because we want something else. In one way or another, we do not keep God's regulations.

Since we are lawbreakers, God's law is against us. It is our enemy; it stands opposed

to us. The list of God's laws is also a list of
our sins. Every one of God's regulations
is another reminder that we have sinned
against a holy God. So this is the hand-signed
bill that the Bible has in mind when it speaks
of "the written code." It is a record of the
infinite debt we owe to God because we have
broken His law.

By now we can see clearly what was
nailed to the cross of Christ along with
Jesus Himself and with the notice of His
kingship. It was a bill showing the charges
we had run up by breaking God's law. It
was a legal note showing that we owed an
infinite debt to God because of our sin. This
certificate of debt had our own signature at
the bottom. And since "the wages of sin is
death" (Rom. 6:23), we had signed our own
death warrant.

THE DEBT CANCELED

The triumph of the cross is that God crucified
the certificate of our debt to His law. He took
away "the written code, with its regulations,
that was against us and that stood opposed
to us... nailing it to the cross" (Col. 2:14).

When our I.O.U. was nailed to the cross
with Christ, all of our sins were forgiven. Our

debt was cleared. As the Bible puts it, God "canceled the written code." In the Greek original, the word "canceled" means "to blot out" or "to wipe away." The idea is that the debt we once owed to God because of our sin has been completely erased.

The triumph of the cross is that God canceled the entire debt of our sin by nailing it to the cross with Christ. He forgave all our sins when Jesus was crucified. Since each and every one of our sins was nailed to the cross with Christ, the entire amount of our debt has been cleared. There are no outstanding charges.

The triumph of the cross over sin is beautifully expressed in a verse from a famous hymn by Horatio G. Spafford. The events of Spafford's life were tragic. In November 1873 he sent his wife and four daughters to Europe on board the French ocean liner *Ville du Havre*. During the Atlantic passage, the steamer collided with another ship and most of the passengers were lost at sea. Among them were Spafford's daughters, although his wife was rescued.

Spafford booked passage on the next available ship. As the vessel neared the spot where his daughters had drowned, he wrote the hymn, "It Is Well with My Soul." Even in grief Spafford was able to take comfort in the triumph of the cross:

> My sin—O the bliss of this glorious thought!—
> My sin, not in part, but the whole,
> Is nailed to the cross and I bear it no more;
> Praise the Lord, praise the Lord, O my soul!

As he wrote these words, Spafford was remembering the second chapter of Colossians, where the Bible says that God forgave the whole debt of our sin by nailing it to the cross.[2]

A PUBLIC SPECTACLE

In the cross of Christ, God not only triumphed over sin, but He also triumphed over Satan. Satan was such an old enemy, and the cross was such a great triumph, that God could not keep this victory to Himself. After explaining how God nailed our sins to the cross, the Bible goes on to say that "having disarmed the powers and authorities, he made a public spectacle of them, triumphing over them by the cross" (v. 15).

Here again it helps to know something about ancient Roman culture. When a general returned home after winning a great war victory, he led a public procession through

---

2. Lindsay L. Terry, *Devotionals from Famous Hymn Stories* (Grand Rapids, MI: Baker, 1986), pp. 11-12.

the streets of Rome. Following in his train were the prisoners he had seized in battle. The general made a public spectacle of his captives because prisoners of war were the proof of total victory.

God did the same thing to Satan on the cross. Satan had been waging war against God for millennia. The earthly battle between heaven and hell was first joined in the Garden of Eden, where Satan tempted Eve to commit the first sin. Ever since then, Satan has tried to destroy God's people by leading them further into sin. He watched with uncontained glee as human beings fell more and more helplessly into debt. He knew that we would never be able to pay what we owed to God for breaking His law.

But there was one thing that Satan forgot to include in his calculations. He did not count on the triumph of the cross. He did not know that Jesus Christ would pay the full price for sin by dying on the cross. He could not see that when Jesus was crucified, the infinite debt we owe to God would be nailed there with him. By the time Satan realized that the cross was the triumph of God rather than the death of God, it was too late.

The Bible says that when God nailed our sins to the cross, he "disarmed the powers and authorities" (v. 15). "Powers and authorities" refers to Satan and his demons. For a time God allowed them to hold the power of sin and the authority of death over God's people. But their power and authority were neutralized on the cross. The Puritan Matthew Henry (1662-1714) put it like this: "The devil and all the powers of hell were conquered and disarmed by the dying Redeemer."[3] When Christ died on the cross, the enemies of God lost the power of sin and the authority of death.

Thus, the crucifixion of Jesus Christ was an exhibition of God's victory over Satan: "Having disarmed the powers and authorities, he made a public spectacle of them, triumphing over them by the cross" (v. 15). Like a mighty general, God conquered the devil and all his demons through the cross. Then He put them on public display. The cross was God's victory parade. It showed that God had triumphed over sin and over Satan by nailing our debts to the cross.

The cross is God's triumph. It is also a triumph for us if we trust in Jesus Christ for salvation. The Reverend Ed King explained the triumph of the cross when he preached

---

3. Matthew Henry, *Matthew Henry's Commentary on the Whole Bible*, 6 vols. (New York: Revell, 1983), vol. 6, in loc.

at the funeral of James Chaney, an African-American peace worker murdered by the Ku Klux Klan in August of 1964. King knew that the Klan used its cross for evil purposes, but he wanted to reclaim the triumphant cross of Christ. "The cross is not a burned cross," he preached. "It is the one cross of Calvary that is stained with the blood of Jesus, God's Son. God gave his Son for all of us and this is the cross that we follow—the cross that means victory."[4]

---

4. Ed King, "Transcription of Eulogies for James Chaney, August 7, 1964" (University of Virginia: The Project on Lived Theology), http://archives.livedtheology.org/node/1404.

6 The Humility of the Cross

"And being found in appearance as a man, he humbled himself and became obedient to death— even death on a cross!"

PHILIPPIANS 2:8

Jesus Christ began at the very top of a great parabola. Being in very nature God and enjoying all the glories of His deity, He was as high as He could be. Then He curved down, down towards humanity. He ungrasped the glories of His deity, emptied Himself, took the very nature of a servant, was made in human likeness, and embraced the humility of the manger.

THE HUMILITY OF THE MANGER

The downward swoop of this parabola brought the Son of God to earth from heaven. Since eternity past, He had always enjoyed the privileges and prerogatives of His divinity. But He took a trajectory of humility, lowering Himself to become a human being. He did not use His equality with God as an excuse for avoiding the incarnation, but did just the reverse.

Jesus Christ was a man in every respect. He was fashioned and constructed as a human being. Underneath His human skin were human bones and human organs, with human blood pumping through human veins. If you had been in the cave where Jesus was born, you could have laid your hand on the baby Jesus and felt His chest go up and down as He breathed the night air of Bethlehem. Mary and Joseph had to feed, burp, and even change Jesus. When they took Him in their arms, they held a living, breathing, wiggling baby.

All this was necessary for Jesus to become the Savior of the world. He had to become one of us in order to save us. "Since man had sinned," wrote the Reformer Zacharias Ursinus, "it was necessary for man to make satisfaction for sin."[1] Or, in the words of Augustine, who perhaps was the greatest

---

1. Zacharias Ursinus, *Commentary on the Heidelberg Catechism*, trans. G.W. Williard (1852; repr. Phillipsburg, NJ: Presbyterian & Reformed, 1985), p. 85.

theologian of the early church, "The very same nature was to be assumed, which was to be delivered."[2]

The humility of Jesus Christ was totally unprecedented. It was an absolute reversal of the values of this world—a new departure in world ethics. "He humbled himself," the Scripture says, indicating a voluntary humility. Just as the Son of God emptied Himself and made Himself nothing (Phil. 2:7), so also he made *Himself* humble. The humiliation of Jesus Christ was an act of willing condescension and voluntary self-renunciation.

We easily forget how radical Christ's example of humility was and is. The ancient heathen philosophers despised humility. For them it was not a virtue, but a vice. Pride was commended, whereas humility was castigated as a sign of weakness and cowardice. For pagans in the time of Christ, humility was the sniveling disposition of a coward. Jesus thus reversed the values of ancient culture and offered humanity a radically different way to live: the way of humility.

---

2. Augustine, quoted in Ursinus, *Commentary on the Heidelberg Catechism*, p. 86.

HUMBLE UNTO DEATH

If we were to page through the Gospels, we could identify many examples of the humility of Jesus Christ. But as he traced the parabola of redemption in its downward arc, Paul contented himself with Christ's single greatest act of humility: He "become obedient unto death ."

Here Paul answers a question that was posed by the haunting lyrics of a popular 1995 song by Joan Osborne that probed the possibility of the incarnation. "What if God was one of us?" Osborne crooned. "Just the same as one of us. Just a slob like one of us. Just a stranger on the bus, trying to make his way home, just back to heaven all alone."

What if God *was* one of us? What would it have been like for Him to participate in all of the tedium and banality of human existence? Actually, there is no need to speculate. No "ifs" about it: God *did* become one of us. We can read all about it in the most thoroughly attested historical documents from the ancient world: the Gospels of the New Testament. Nor was Jesus trying to make His way back home all on His own. He was strengthened by the Holy Spirit and supported by His intimate fellowship with God the Father every step of the way.

But a deeper problem with Osborne's song, from a biblical standpoint, is that the Jesus it presents is not humiliated enough. Osborne's Jesus is a pitiable figure. We see him lonely on the bus, friendless and forlorn in a fallen world. The melancholy man seems forsaken by God, uncertain of his eternal destiny, abandoned to work out his own salvation. But the humiliation of His true incarnation was much worse! His parabola swept much lower than a crowded bus on a city street. The obedience of Christ was an obedience all the way to the death.

This statement does not refer primarily to the duration of Christ's obedience. It is true that Jesus obeyed God's law all the way through His life, and that He obeyed His Father right up until the moment of His death. But what "obedience unto death" chiefly expresses is the *degree* of Christ's obedience. Dying on the cross was obedience to the nth degree, to the absolute extremity of death.

This superlative obedience demonstrated both the deity and the humanity of Jesus Christ. On the one hand, offering His body for death demonstrated His deity. Death cannot be an act of obedience for mere human beings. It is inevitable for us because we are mortals. Whether we willingly submit to death or not, we all must die. Only God the Son, as very God of very God, could submit Himself to death in an act of voluntary obedience.

At the same time, the obedience of Christ unto death demonstrated His humanity. Elsewhere the Scripture says, "During the days of Jesus' life on earth, he offered up prayers and petitions with loud cries and tears to the one who could save him from death, and he was heard because of his reverent submission. Although he was a son, he learned obedience from what he suffered" (Heb. 5:7-8). These verses offer us a rare glimpse of the emotional life of Jesus Christ, which included loud cries and tears to His heavenly Father for deliverance from death. Jesus Christ learned obedience through suffering.

Jesus Christ could have refused the way of the cross. Once He had the chance to survey His surroundings, to see things with human eyes, and to experience earthly suffering in His own skin, He could have chosen to exchange His humility back again for glory. Indeed, this was the temptation that Satan presented to Jesus: "The devil took him to a very high mountain and showed him all the kingdoms of the world and their splendor. 'All this I will give you,' he said, 'if you will bow down and worship me'" (Matt. 4:8-9). Satan offered Jesus a road to glory that did not pass through Calvary.

Jesus rejected that easy road. He rejected it because there could be no salvation from sin without atonement for sin. There could be no redemption without crucifixion. So Jesus Christ chose to follow the downward path of the parabola of redemption. He was obedient unto death.

Even Death on a Cross

There is more. Across the long centuries we can still hear the amazement in Paul's voice as he says, "Even death on a cross!" Jesus chose to undergo not only the humility of the manger, but also the humility of the cross.

John Chrysostom (c. 347-407) was among the greatest preachers of the early church. His pulpit ministry in Constantinople was so magnificent that he was called "Golden Tongue" (which is what "Chrysostom" means in Greek). This great orator was rarely at a loss for words, yet when he came to this phrase in Philippians 2 he said, "words fail me."[3]

---

3. John Chrysostom, *Homilies on Philippians*, http://orthodox churchfathers.com/fathers/npnf113/npnf1149.htm.

Words do fail us. Yet we need to know what Jesus suffered on the cross for our sake. Doctor C. Truman Davis describes the effects of crucifixion as follows:

The cross is placed on the ground and the exhausted man is quickly thrown backwards with his shoulders against the wood. The legionnaire feels for the depression at the front of the wrist. He drives a heavy, square wrought-iron nail through the wrist and deep into the wood. Quickly he moves to the other side and repeats the action, being careful not to pull the arms too tightly, but to allow some flex and movement. The cross is then lifted into place.

The left foot is pressed backward against the right foot, and with both feet extended, toes down, a nail is driven through the arch of each, leaving the knees flexed. The victim is now crucified. As he slowly sags down with more weight on the nails in the wrists, excruciating, fiery pain shoots along the fingers and up the arms to explode in the brain—the nails in the wrists are putting pressure on the median nerves. As he pushes himself upward to avoid this stretching torment, he places the full weight on the nail through his feet. Again he feels the searing agony of the nail tearing through the nerves between the bones of his feet.

As the arms fatigue, cramps sweep through the muscles, knotting them in deep, relentless, throbbing pain. With these cramps comes the inability to push himself upward to breathe. Air can be drawn into the lungs but not exhaled. He fights to raise himself in order to get even one small breath. Finally carbon dioxide builds up in the lungs and in the blood stream, and the cramps partially subside. Spasmodically he is able to push himself upward to exhale and bring in life-giving oxygen.

Hours of this limitless pain, cycles of twisting, joint-rending cramps, intermittent partial asphyxiation, searing pain as tissue is torn from his lacerated back as he moves up and down against the rough timber. Then another agony begins: a deep, crushing pain in the chest as the pericardium slowly fills with serum and begins to compress the heart.

It is now almost over—the loss of tissue fluids has reached a critical level—the compressed heart is struggling to pump heavy, thick, sluggish blood into the tissues—the tortured lungs are making a frantic effort to gasp in small gulps of air.

He can feel the chill of death creeping through his tissues...[4]

Yes, words fail us. The Scripture says that "For the joy set before him, Jesus endured the cross" (Heb. 12:2). The cross that Jesus endured was no mere symbol. It was not a pendant dangling cheerfully from the neck, or an icon fixed on the wall. It was sheer torture.

---

4. C. Truman Davis, "A Physician's View of the Crucifixion of Jesus Christ," http://www.cbn.com/SpiritualLife/ OnlineDiscipleship/easter/A_Physician%27s_View_of_ the_Crucifixion_of_Jesus_Christ.aspx.

Here we have reached the very bottom of the parabola of redemption. The humility of the manger was only the beginning. When the Son of God became a man He started down the parabolic path of obedience that swept from the manger down, down to the cross.

No wonder Paul was amazed! Even though he had walked with the Lord for many years, thinking often of the cross of Christ and suffering many trials himself, he could scarcely believe that Jesus endured such humiliation. For in those days, crucifixion was the most despised of all deaths.

As we saw earlier in this book, the cross was despised by pagans. In Plato's *Republic,* Glaucon sets out to prove to Socrates how a just man could be proved to be just. In order to prove his goodness, the just man would have to suffer every insult and endure every kind of hardship. Here is how Glaucon concludes his description of the injustices he must face: "The just man in those circumstances will be scourged, racked, chained, have his eyes burnt out; at last, after every kind of misery, he will be crucified..."[5]

---

5. Plato, *The Republic,* trans. Francis MacDonald Cornford (New York: Oxford University Press, 1954), pp. 45-47 (II,

Crucifixion would be the ultimate proof that this man was perfect, for it was the worst of all possible deaths.

The idea that crucifixion was the nadir of humiliation was widespread in the Roman world, where decapitation was considered preferable to crucifixion. The cross was reserved for the scum of humanity: slaves and violent criminals, malefactors and traitors. Perhaps Paul specifies that Jesus was a servant in Philippians 2 in order to show that He was, in fact, eligible for the cross.

If crucifixion was an obscenity to the pagans, it was a curse to the Jews. According to the Law of Moses—as we have seen—to be hung on a tree was to be accursed by God and excommunicated from the people of God (Deut. 21:22-23). A man crucified was beyond the possibility of redemption. Thus Jesus bore more than the pain of crucifixion and the vilification of pagans; He also suffered a divine curse against human sin.

Given this cultural and religious context, one wonders if there was a time when the cross was an obstacle to Paul's faith in the gospel. As both a Roman and a Jew,

360D-362E).

he would have had a deep and instinctive revulsion to honoring any man who had died on a cross. This may help to explain the detailed attention he gives to the meaning of the cross in his preaching and writing. It certainly explains his utter amazement that the Son of God would actually die on a cross. If death on a tree was an accursed thing, then how could the Lord of Glory die in that way? A crucified Messiah!? This would have been an oxymoron for Paul before his conversion—a logical impossibility. When he later wrote that Christ crucified was a "stumbling block to the Jews" (1 Cor. 1:23), he was speaking from his own prior confusion over the paradox of the cross.

Yet Paul did not set aside the Old Testament, for he knew that whatever the Bible said was true. Nor did he set aside the historical facts of the life of Jesus, for he was an eyewitness of the risen Christ. Instead, the apostle wrestled with the text until he understood what it was saying about the historical facts. What he discovered is recorded in Scripture: "Christ redeemed us from the curse of the law by becoming a curse for us, as it is written: 'Cursed is everyone who is hung on a tree'" (Gal. 3:13).

THE HUMILITY OF THE CHRISTIAN

Jesus Christ humbled Himself and was obedient unto death, even death on a cross. He bore the curse of that cross for our salvation, enduring its pain and scorning its shame (see Heb. 12:2).

Anyone who has not yet come to Christ for forgiveness is still subject to the curse that He bore on the cross. Unless we turn away from our rebellion against God, the curse of God hangs over us like a death sentence, and we are liable to bear that curse in our own person. If God did not spare His own Son from His curse against sin (see Rom. 8:32), then why would He spare us from that curse? It is only at the cross of Christ that we can escape the curse our sins deserve.

If we have taken our sins to the cross of Christ, what then? Philippians 2:8 is primarily about what the cross means for Christ, not what it means for us. This verse is about the suffering and the shame that Jesus endured on the cross as an act of humility. It is first and foremost about how low Jesus Christ was willing to go in working out our salvation.

But once we see the attitude of Christ towards the cross, how humbly He endured the shame of the cross, then we can also see how our attitude should be like His attitude. The cross brings us to this practical exhortation:

> Your attitude should be the same as that of Christ Jesus. Do nothing out of selfish ambition or vain conceit, but in humility consider others better than yourselves. Each of you should look not only to your own interests, but also to the interests of others. (Phil. 2:5, 3-4)

Few of us have difficulty remembering to take care of ourselves. Indeed, we rarely look very far beyond our own interests. Often we do the opposite of what the Scripture says and consider ourselves better than others. But Paul tells us to follow a pattern of Christ-like humility and put other people first.

When this exhortation has its way with us, it will turn our instincts and priorities upside down. At the cross we see how much lower we still have to go. There remains too much pride in our humility; even our acts of compassion can be self-serving. God is calling us to exercise instead the self-sacrificing, self-emptying, self-suffering, self-denying humility of Jesus Christ on the cross.

7 ⌐The Boast of the Cross⌐

"May I never boast except in the cross,
of our Lord Jesus Christ."

GALATIANS 6:14

There is something curious about boasting. Despite the fact that nobody likes a braggart, everybody brags anyway. People boast about anything and everything: grandchildren, bank accounts, waistlines, bowling averages, travel plans, accomplishments, sometimes even their indiscretions.

In the 1990s an outlandish boast appeared on television. Most commercials involve a fair amount of bragging anyway, but this one reached a new low in advertising. An automobile company proudly announced the "most impressive safety advance ever ... a car that can save your soul."

God Forbid!

The apostle Paul never would have boasted about an automobile. Or anything else, for that matter. "May I never boast," he wrote to the Galatians (6:14). "Far be it from me to make a boast." Or, more literally, "God forbid that I should ever boast!"

Since Paul was a scholar of the Old Testament, he knew that the Bible forbids boasting. "This is what the Lord says," according to the prophet Jeremiah: "Let not the wise man boast of his wisdom or the strong man boast of his strength or the rich man boast of his riches" (Jer. 9:23). If a man cannot boast about his brainpower, his muscle power, or his buying power, what can he boast about? Nothing at all. King Solomon wisely gave this warning: "Let another praise you, and not your own mouth; someone else, and not your own lips" (Prov. 27:2). In other words, let someone else blow your horn!

Boasting is never attractive. The worst boasting of all is bragging about one's religious accomplishments. Yet this is exactly what some people were doing in the days of Paul. Many of the first Christians were Jews by birth, so they had been circumcised in their infancy. Circumcision was the Old

Testament sign of belonging to God's people. If a Gentile man wanted to join the Jewish community, he had to be circumcised. Some early Christians thought that circumcision was still a requirement for membership in the community of the saved. Anyone who wants to become a true follower of Jesus Christ, they said, also has to get circumcised in the Old Testament fashion.

Although it seems strange to modern ears, the pro-circumcision people were so proud of being circumcised that they started bragging about it. The more Gentiles they could persuade to get circumcised, the more they bragged. Here is what the Bible says about them: "They want you to be circumcised that they may boast about your flesh" (Gal. 6:13). Talk about being holier than thou!

Religious people do not brag about circumcision the way they once did, but we still find plenty of things to boast about. We brag about our church attendance, our converts, our style of worship, our devotional habits, our political commitments, or our particular brand of theology. In one way or another we find subtle ways to call attention to how spiritual we are. Frankly, one of the main reasons some people are so hostile toward the church is that Christians can be so smug.

Paul himself had plenty of religious things to boast about. On one occasion he listed the highlights of his spiritual résumé: "Circumcised on the eighth day, of the people of Israel, of the tribe of Benjamin, a Hebrew of Hebrews; in regard to the law, a Pharisee; as for zeal, persecuting the church; as for legalistic righteousness, faultless" (Phil. 3:5-6). What more could anyone ask for? Paul had all the right connections. He came from a good family, attended the best schools, and believed the most orthodox theology.

The apostle had as much to boast about as anyone else, if he had wanted to. But when Paul came to know Jesus Christ, he realized that he had nothing to boast about at all. All his religious accomplishments amounted to was a load of rubbish (Phil. 3:8). God forbid that he should boast about any of them!

A Most Unusual Obsession

There is only one thing in the whole universe worth boasting about. The Bible allows for a single exception: "May I never boast except in the cross of our Lord Jesus Christ" (Gal. 6:14).

The surprising thing about this boast is that in the ancient world crucifixion was nothing to boast about. Earlier we noted that the cross was an offense to the Romans and a curse to the Jews. The New Testament scholar F. F. Bruce concludes that the

> object of Paul's present boasting was, by all ordinary standards of his day, the most ignoble of all objects—a matter of unrelieved shame, not of boasting. It is difficult, after sixteen centuries and more during which the cross has been a sacred symbol, to realize the unspeakable horror and loathing which the very mention or thought of the cross provoked in Paul's day. The word *crux* was unmentionable in polite Roman society (Cicero, *Pro Rabirio* 16); even when one was being condemned to death by crucifixion the sentence used an archaic formula which served as a sort of euphemism: *arbori infelici suspendito*, "hang him on the unlucky tree" (Cicero, ibid. 13). In the eastern provinces of the empire the Greek word *stauros* ("cross") must have inspired comparable dread and disgust to its Latin equivalent.[1]

Thus, it was shocking for Paul even to mention the cross, let alone boast about it. If anything, one would expect the first Christians to *deny* that Jesus died on the cross. Or at most, if they were honest, to admit this fact only with the greatest reluctance.

Far from being reluctant, however, Paul was eager to boast about the cross. As John Stott ex-

---

1   F. F. Bruce, *The Epistle to the Galatians: A Commentary on the Greek Text*, New International Greek Testament Commentary (Grand Rapids, MI: Eerdmans, 1982), p. 271.

plains, "That which the average Roman citizen regarded as an object of shame, disgrace and even disgust was for Paul his pride, boasting and glory."[2] Indeed, the English word "boast" is hardly strong enough to express his attitude about the cross. As Stott goes on to say, "There is no exact equivalent in the English language to *kauchaomai*. It means to boast in, glory in, trust in, rejoice in, revel in, live for. The object of our boast or 'glory' fills our horizons, engrosses our attention, and absorbs our time and energy. In a word, our 'glory' is our obsession."[3]

DEAD TO SIN, ALIVE TO GOD'S LOVE

Why are Christians so obsessed with the cross? Why do they revel in it? What makes it something to boast about?

First, the cross means the death of sin. Paul's full statement runs as follows: "May I never boast except in the cross of our Lord Jesus Christ, through which the world has been crucified to me, and I to the world" (v. 14). By "the world" is meant the world without God, in all its vanity. The world represents the tyranny of sin over humanity. Every human being is

---

2. John R. W. Stott, *The Cross of Christ* (Downers Grove, IL: InterVarsity, 1986), p. 349.

3. Ibid.

born in sin and continues to sin. Even Paul himself had been in bondage to sin—enslaved to the world, with all its wicked ways.

The crucifixion of Jesus Christ, however, struck a mortal blow to sin's worldly power. As we saw earlier, it was as if sin itself was nailed to the cross with Jesus (Col. 2:13-15). Christ died on the cross not only to atone for sin, but ultimately to bring it to an end.

Christians boast in the cross because it means the beginning of the end of our sin. Sin no longer holds us in its death-grip. More and more, we are becoming dead to the temptations and enticements of sin. One day, when Christ returns, we will be done with it once and for all.

Another reason to boast about the cross of Christ is because it is the greatest demonstration of God's love. It shows the love of God the Father, who gave up His only Son as a sacrifice to save His people. Therefore, to glory in the cross is to glory in God's love.

A father's love is always something to boast about. This is true at the human level. A father once put a note in his son's lunch box. It was just a simple note saying, "Hope you have a nice day at school. See you when I get home. Love, Dad."

When the boy returned home from school, his mother noticed that the note was still tucked into his lunch box, unopened. Apparently the boy hadn't noticed it, so she pulled it out and handed it to him. He took the note, read it, and began to cry. When his mother hugged him and asked what was the matter, he said, "I didn't realize Dad loved me that much."[44] Such is the power of a father's love.

A father's love is all the more powerful when it is divine. The cross of Christ shows the children of God how deeply they are loved by their Father in heaven. Boasting about that cross is a way of saying, "See, my Heavenly Father loves me!"

Understand that the boast of the cross is not an exclusive boast. Usually what makes boasting so unpleasant is that the boaster has something to boast about and you don't! But the boast of the cross is not intended to keep people on the outside. Anyone may come to the cross. Jesus invites everyone to come to Him, to have sins forgiven, and to receive eternal life. Boasting in his cross is open to anyone who will receive Him.

---

4.   Recounted in Gary and Anne Marie Ezzo, *Growing Kids God's Way: Biblical Ethics for Parenting* (Chatsworth, CA: Growing Families International, 1993), pp. 95-96.

THE WONDROUS CROSS

One of the best-loved hymns of the church is based on the words we have been studying: "May I never boast except in the cross of our Lord Jesus Christ, through which the world has been crucified to me, and I to the world" (v. 14). The hymn, which is entitled, "When I Survey the Wondrous Cross," was written by Isaac Watts (1674-1748), and it is a boast about the only thing in all the world worth boasting about.

First, the hymn rules out all other forms of boasting as God-forbidden:

> When I survey the wondrous cross
> On which the Prince of glory died,
> My richest gain I count but loss,
> And pour contempt on all my pride.
> Forbid it, Lord, that I should boast,
> Save in the death of Christ, my God;
> All the vain things that charm me most—
> I sacrifice them to His blood.

Then the hymn-writer speaks of the love that flowed down from the cross, before ending with a prayer of total commitment to Christ. If we are wise, we will make this commitment our own:

> See from His head, His hands, His feet,
> Sorrow and love flow mingled down;
> Did e'er such love and sorrow meet,
> Or thorns compose so rich a crown?

Were the whole realm of nature mine,
That were a present far too small;
Love so amazing, so divine,
Demands my soul, my life, my all.

Also available from Christian Focus...

14 WORDS FROM JESUS

JAMES MONTGOMERY BOICE
PHILIP GRAHAM RYKEN

ISBN 978-1-78191-205-8

14 Words from Jesus

JAMES MONTGOMERY BOICE AND PHILIP G. RYKEN

These inspirational readings probe Christ's seven words from the cross and equally significant, seven words from the risen Lord, after His death. These words highlight the glory of Calvary, the heart of God and how wonderfully Jesus understood that His death and resurrection was to be effective in bringing into being atonement from sin for those seeking forgiveness.

It is a delight to me personally and a privilege for the Christian world generally to have these examples of their Biblical ministry made available by Christian Focus.

Eric Alexander
Conference speaker and formerly minister St George's Tron, Glasgow for 20 years.

James Montgomery Boice (1938-2000) was pastor of Tenth Presbyterian Church, Philadelphia from 1968 until his death in 2000. He served as Chairman of the International Council on Biblical Inerrancy and was a founding member of the Alliance of Confessing Evangelicals. He was a prolific author and published over 50 works.

Dr Ryken became President of Wheaton College in July 2010. Prior to that he was Senior Minister of Tenth Presbyterian Church, Philadelphia, Pennsylvania. He is also a prolific author and a council member of the Alliance of Confessing Evangelicals, blogging on their website www.reformation21.org.

Christian Focus Publications

Our mission statement –

STAYING FAITHFUL
In dependence upon God we seek to impact the world
through literature faithful to His infallible Word, the Bible.
Our aim is to ensure that the Lord Jesus Christ is presented
as the only hope to obtain forgiveness of sin, live a useful
life and look forward to heaven with Him.

Our Books are published in four imprints:

CHRISTIAN FOCUS

popular works including biographies, commentaries, basic
doctrine and Christian living.

CHRISTIAN HERITAGE

books representing some of
the best material from the rich
heritage of the church.

MENTOR

books written at a level suitable
for Bible College and seminary
students, pastors, and other serious readers. The imprint includes
commentaries, doctrinal studies,
examination of current issues and
church history.

CF4•K

children's books for quality
Bible teaching and for all age
groups: Sunday school curricu-
lum, puzzle and activity books;
personal and family devotional
titles, biographies and inspirational stories – Because you are
never too young to know Jesus!

Christian Focus Publications Ltd,
Geanies House, Fearn, Ross-shire,
IV20 1TW, Scotland, United Kingdom.
www.christianfocus.com